FROM EXHAUSTED TO ENERGIZED

A Self-Care Guide for Women
Affected by a Loved One's Addiction.
Four Easy Steps to Overcome Stress and
Stop the Endless Cycle of Going to Bed
Exhausted and Waking up Depleted,
so You Can Begin to Thrive
Instead of Just Survive.

SANDY SONIER

BALBOA.PRESS
A DIVISION OF HAY HOUSE

Balboa Press books may be ordered through booksellers or by contacting:

Balboa Press
A Division of Hay House
1663 Liberty Drive
Bloomington, IN 47403
www.balboapress.com
844-682-1282

Because of the dynamic nature of the Internet, any web addresses or
links contained in this book may have changed since publication and
may no longer be valid. The views expressed in this work are solely those
of the author and do not necessarily reflect the views of the publisher,
and the publisher hereby disclaims any responsibility for them.

The author of this book does not dispense medical advice or prescribe
the use of any technique as a form of treatment for physical, emotional,
or medical problems without the advice of a physician, either directly
or indirectly. The intent of the author is only to offer information
of a general nature to help you in your quest for emotional and
spiritual well-being. In the event you use any of the information in
this book for yourself, which is your constitutional right, the author
and the publisher assume no responsibility for your actions.

Print information available on the last page.

ISBN: 978-1-9822-7996-7 (sc)
ISBN: 978-1-9822-7995-0 (e)

Library of Congress Control Number: 2022902975

Balboa Press rev. date: 03/08/2022

CONTENTS

FOREWORD

There are literally thousands of books out there about health, fitness, mindfulness and stress. But, most of the time, they are experts writing for other experts, and the 'regular person' is left dazzled by buzzwords and jargon, with no clue how to actually make changes that HELP. Not anymore.

Sandy Sonier has taken her library of knowledge and understanding and used it to write this simple guide to health and wellness that is easy to read and allows readers to instantly implement her tips and suggestions. The experiences she shares around her own struggles with health and wellness make her the ideal writer to follow, as she leads you through a full mind/body transformation that could literally save your life.

What??

Well, think about it. Stress is a daily issue in our lives – we all experience some. Stress, over time, can lead to other issues like ulcers, insomnia, even heart disease, and the more our body is under stress, the worse our health becomes. In the US, diabetes, heart disease and cancer are at all-time highs, and more and more of us are either touched by it or know someone who has been. How many people in your circle struggle with stress or are overweight and unhealthy? A huge number of diseases are caused by stress, poor diet and nutrition, or weight issues, opening the door to even worse health conditions down the line. Almost everyone today experiences stress on a regular basis. Most people try to 'tough' their way through their struggles, but with a few simple lifestyle changes, you can let go of the stress, create a healthier body and calmer mind. Wouldn't that feel great?

Your family doctor may not have a lot of tools to offer to combat stress and to properly care for your body. It's up to people to educate themselves, so it's great that you found your way here.

If you're having a hard time seeing how food, sleep and managing stress can make a difference to your physical and mental quality of life, think of it as 'garbage in, garbage out'. The better you eat, the better you feel, and the less you will struggle with health over your lifetime. The better you sleep, the less stress you will experience on a daily basis. The less stress you feel, the healthier your heart and body will become.

Sandy shared with me how important it was to her to keep this book simple and straightforward, and I think she's done an amazing job with that. Information only has value if it is understandable, relatable, and easy to add into your life, and I promise you, this is.

As my student, client and friend, I'm immeasurably proud of Sandy and the work she's done to make this book something anyone can use to improve their health. And I'm very proud of you, the reader, for taking it to heart and putting it into action.

Maybe one book can't change the world, but it could change YOUR world, through improved health, happiness and vitality, and think of all the lives you can impact by setting an example. So… maybe it can!

So, come on. Get busy reading and doing, and let's change the world, one better choice at a time.

Jana Beeman, Certified Master Coach Trainer, CHHP, CHT, MS

ACKNOWLEDGEMENTS

There are so many people who have come and gone in my life that have had a positive impact on me, including many friends and a very special grade-school teacher, Mrs. Linda Williams. Her love for her "Kids" had a huge impact on me, at a very young age, and we kept in touch until she passed away in November 2021. Thank you all.

A loving "Thank You" to my husband, my two sons, my dad and brother who have always supported me and encouraged me to keep following my dreams. It is true; we do reap what we sow.

A heart-felt "Thank You" goes out to my coach/mentor/friend, Jana Beeman. We met when I was enrolled in my wellness coaching class. Jana is an amazing coach. She boosted my self-confidence and taught me the importance of authenticity and that I am enough. She also introduced me to the term, *highly sensitive people (HSP),* which has helped me understand myself more and how to coach other HSP.

I would like to thank my Partylite family of nine years. These ladies were positive and inspirational role models. They helped me step outside of my comfort zone. I believe this is where I gained many leadership skills as well. When you surround yourself with outstanding leaders, it eventually rubs off. It was at a Partylite Convention where I heard motivational speaker Jack Canfield and author of <u>Chicken Soup for the Soul</u> speak. His presentation taught me how to set achievable goals and the power of perseverance.

I would like to thank my Al-Anon family for giving me hope in my darkest days and for sharing their experience and strength. This amazing program helped me reconnect with my Higher Power and my spirituality.

DEDICATION

My mom was my biggest supporter. She was my rock. She showed me unconditional love and was always there for me. She was very good at listening without interruption and always shared words of wisdom or encouragement. She taught me courage, kindness, compassion, patience, and how to love unconditionally.

My mom is my inspiration for this book. She was fun-loving. She was a giver. She liked to help others and put them first, but that meant her needs came last. She didn't learn about boundaries, so she had a hard time saying, "No" or keeping people from taking advantage of her. I believe the caregiver in her and lack of self-care, eventually resulted in lung cancer, which took her life too soon.

When she passed away six years ago, she took a big piece of me with her. I miss her every day; her laughter, her hugs, her listening ear, and her smile. We had a very close and loving relationship. As I grew into adulthood, she became my best friend.

I am my mother's daughter. I can hear her voice sometimes when I talk or I hear her laughter when I laugh. I like to help others and I find it easier to give than receive, as she did. She loved animals. She treated her dogs like children. I do the same. She was an avid reader of murder mysteries. I too am an avid reader and started out reading murder mysteries, but my interests changed and now I read health and wellness books.

This book is dedicated in loving memory of my mom, Coraline, known as "Grandma Corny" to her grandkids. I am so grateful that I was able to tell her how much I loved her and how much I appreciated her before she passed.

INTRODUCTION

Welcome to your self-care guide. I wanted to write this guide to share how you can take small, simple steps to overcome day-to-day stress and learn to embrace self-care without feeling guilty. My wellness philosophy is ***Self-care is not selfish, but essential***. When you take care of yourself, you will have the energy to be the person you want to be and available to those when needed. This guide is to be used with patience, gentleness and self-love. When you practice these tips and steps, they will become healthy habits, and you will start to thrive instead of just survive.

I grew up in an alcoholic family, with a brother who became an alcoholic at age 17. Since alcoholism runs in my family, I was not overly surprised when my oldest son told us he was addicted to prescription opioids age 27 and then soon became addicted to alcohol. My wellness journey has brought me from feelings of low self-esteem, co-dependency, guilt and total exhaustion to more energy, peace, joy and better overall health and wellbeing.

My life's journey has also brought me to my passion, which is educating and empowering women affected by a loved one's drinking or addiction, to overcome mental and physical exhaustion from taking care of everyone and everything, so they too can experience more energy, peace and joy.

This self-care guide includes tips that I share with my clients and use myself to find more peace and overcome day-to-day stress, as well as resources from my wellness certification, and from the many books I have read. I am a certified holistic wellness master coach and not a counselor or nutritionist. I would recommend that if you are under the care of a physician or counselor that you talk with them before you start any new "diet" or exercise program. Please keep in mind as you read this guide that what works for one individual may not work for you, so you may need to experiment with different tips to find what works best for you.

There are many things that may be causing stress. The first step is to recognize what is causing your stress by asking yourself these questions.

Am I overbooked and doing too many things?

Am I focused on quality nutrition, so I have the energy to handle day-to-day stressors?

Am I getting enough quality sleep?

Am I taking time out to relax and care for myself?

Are my thoughts running non-stop?

Once you determine what is causing your stress, you can turn to the chapter to learn about its importance and what steps you can take to find relief.

ONE

Stress Less for More
Happiness

Stress? What stress? If you grew up around alcoholism or perhaps married into it, then you are very familiar with stress. Today, we are bombarded with stress environmentally, physically and emotionally. Environmental stress includes air and water pollution and chemicals in our food. Physical stress includes muscle aches and pain or illness. Emotional stress includes depression, anxiety or mental fog. I will be talking more about emotional stress in this chapter.

Everyone reacts to stress differently. However, everyone makes cortisol in their body, and stress is directly linked to cortisol. Cortisol is our main stress hormone that activates our fight or flight response. It is made in our adrenal glands, which sit directly above each kidney, and its main job is to help us handle stress. A little stress is actually good for us, as it helps us grow. But when our lives are full of stressful events all day long, we end up flooding our bodies with cortisol too often, upsetting our hormone balance and causing illness.

I have spent many days and nights caught up in the web of stressful events. My first memory of a terrible, stressful event happened when I was 16 years old. I was babysitting and received a phone call that my brother, who was 17 years old at the time, was in the hospital after a car accident, getting his stomach pumped from consuming too much alcohol. My heart sank to my stomach, and all I could do was worry. That was the start of his addiction to alcohol and marijuana and my time to figure out how to deal with this stressful situation at home. During the week, I hid in my room doing homework to escape and to study so I would receive all A's to make my parents proud and to not cause any additional stress for them. However, on the weekends, I drank alcohol and partied to escape.

Then my life was turned upside down when my boyfriend went off to college in another state and my parents divorced the same year, which was my senior year of high school. I felt totally abandoned and didn't care much about anything. I almost dropped out of school, like my brother did in his junior year of high school. Thankfully I graduated. I can remember during my adolescent and teen years, I had constant stomach aches and headaches. Now I can see that stress played a role in my digestive problems and headaches.

Stress can show up in many ways. It can cause headaches, digestive issues, adrenal fatigue or "burnout", insomnia, high blood pressure, stroke, malnutrition, obesity, anxiety, and depression, just to name a few. How does your body tell you when you are under stress or feeling overwhelmed?

When I reflect on my life, I went through many stressful events that I can't believe I survived. The most stressful event was when I went through two family crises back- to-back. My 28- year -old son was struggling with alcoholism and hospitalizations, at the same time my mom was diagnosed with lung cancer and fighting for her life on a ventilator. Being the dedicated employee that I was, I went into work for a half day, then drove an hour to be with my mom in the hospital. We were told that she would not survive and was not a candidate for any treatment. We had to make the horrible decision to remove her from life support. It was the hardest thing I had ever had to do. I love my mom dearly, and we were very close. I could not bring myself to saying good bye, as good-bye felt so final. Instead, I told her that I am waiting for the day, we say hello again in heaven.

I stayed strong like she taught me. She died just one month after her cancer diagnosis. I am thankful she did not have to suffer. This was by far the most stressful situation I had ever experienced. It was several years later, that this suppressed stress came to the forefront, and I experienced Adrenal fatigue, which showed up as exhaustion. This was my wake- up call for me to really embrace self-care, and it was the start of my wellness journey, which led me to a wellness coaching certification in 2018 and this self-care guide.

So, what is really causing us to have stress in our lives? It is our thoughts that create stress. Did you know that on the average, we have 60,000 thoughts a day? And most of them are not new thoughts. Most of our thoughts are recycled thoughts day after day. We experience the highest level of stress when we feel we have no control over something. I will discuss these recycled thoughts more in chapter 3, where you will learn how to control that crazy brain chatter.

What can you do to start to manage your stress? You can increase your Oxytocin level. Oxytocin is another hormone that we produce, which is referred to as the "Love Hormone". It is an anti-stress hormone, which encourages you to cuddle, hug and nurture. It makes you feel all warm and fuzzy inside.

Here are some simple tips on how to handle stress in a healthy way and produce more Oxytocin.

1. *Go for a walk*- Walking outdoors with nature can improve mood, improve memory, boost your body's ability to battle illness, nurtures creativity, helps with sleep and connects you with your spirituality. I find a walk with nature lifts my spirits and helps me to find gratitude and solve problems.

2. **Exercise**- Any form of exercise may be the number one stress reliever. It has a lot of the same health benefits as walking. My favorite exercise is Jazzercise, which is a mix of dance and weight training to today's music. Find something that you enjoy, so it will become a habit.

3. **Breathe Deeply**- Take a deep breath in while counting to four, hold for a count of four and then release while counting to four. This immediately reduces your stress level.

4. **Drink a cup of chamomile tea**- Chamomile will relax you, while tea will provide antioxidants to ward off free radicals, which cause disease.

5. **Enjoy a warm bath with Epsom salt**- Epsom salt is magnesium sulfate, which has many health benefits, including reducing stress and flushing out toxins.

6. **Do something fun**- Do more of what you love.

7. **Connect with a friend**- We are social beings and need to feel connected. Call a friend for a girl's night out.

8. ***Touch or be touched-*** Hugging, massage, handholding, reflexology and petting your dog or cat, increase your Oxytocin hormone.

9. ***Listen to calming music-*** This can change your brain function to that of meditation. This is great if you have a hard time with mediation.

10. ***Use essential oils-*** Clary sage, jasmine, and orange are a few essential oils that may balance hormones and produce the love hormone. Lavender, cypress, and peppermint essential oils relieve stress. Essential oils can be used in diffusers, in your water, or on your skin. I truly believe in Essential oils and their healing properties. I carry several with me in my purse.

You may not know what brings you joy if you have been so wrapped up in other people's lives. I had to sit down and write a list of those things that I enjoy or used to enjoy. The list above can serve as your new list until you find other things that bring you joy. Whenever I feel life is out of control, I grab my list and pick something fun to do. Remember, one small change can have a big impact on your wellbeing. Once you start to add more joy in your life and produce more Oxytocin than Cortisol, there won't be room for stress, and you will become the winner.

What is one new activity you will start today?

Summary

Stress comes in many forms and many levels. Stress can come from our environment. We can experience physical stress and mental stress. Some of this stress may be out of your control; however, there are many easy steps you can take to reduce the amount of stress in your life. If stress is left unattended, it may lead to headaches, body aches, depression, heart disease, high blood pressure, anxiety, digestive issues, obesity and even death. I know from experience that when I am caught in the web of stress, taking care of myself is the last thing on my mind. I also know that stress will win, if I don't take control. **Remember, self-care is not selfish, it is essential.**

Client testimonial:

> *When I began my coaching program with Sandy, I was very stressed due to lack of time management. I was balancing two careers and jobs, along with wanting and needing to take care of myself and my family. Since I have completed Sandy's program, I have been adding yoga to my daily schedule and I have noticed an incredible change in my*

stress level. Also, I have learned to really manage my time between my two jobs effectively, in a way that creates less stress for me. I have learned very simply, that yes, I can do this! I really benefited from the ability to talk through my challenges and come up with small, yet effective steps to overcome them through the course of my program with Sandy. I highly recommend Sandy to anyone who is struggling with the delicate balance between career, self-care and family life!

Kate

Congratulations on taking the first step of picking up this book to learn how to regain control of your life, so stress is not the winner.

TWO

Is Your Diet Stressing You Out?

Are you getting quality nutrition? Proper nutrition provides the vitamins and nutrients our body needs for energy, to build immunity, combat inflammation and overcome stress. You need quality food to fuel your body and your mind. Eating the right foods may reduce the risk of disease and depression, to name a few.

Growing up, my mom fixed healthy meals, but I remember eating a lot of Little Debbie's snacks, chips, and pizza rolls. These eating habits were passed down to my children, as I was packing these same processed foods in their lunches. As the years passed, I was suffering from daily headaches, mood swings and stomach pain, as well as crippling menstrual cramps. I went to my doctor for the stomach pain, and he diagnosed me with IBS (Irritable Bowel Syndrome). I did not want to spend the rest of my life with this pain, or on medication for these symptoms, so I started reading health books to get to the root cause of my digestive problems and headaches.

I recognized that my symptoms could be related to stress as well as my diet. I discovered that I was an emotional eater. When I was under stress or bored, I would eat candy bars, cookies or brownies. I eventually became addicted to chocolate. I learned that emotional eating was called 'unconscious eating." Unconscious eating is eating because of stress, boredom, anger, sadness, eating in front of the TV, etc. I remember one time when I was eating lunch, while working at my desk, I picked up my pencil and stuck it in my mouth, thinking it was a pretzel. I was able to laugh at myself and realized that I needed to slow down. As for my chocolate addiction, I still eat chocolate, but I switched to 70% or higher dark chocolate and limit myself to two squares daily. I also found other healthy ways to deal with stress, which you will read more about in this book.

In 2009, I joined a wellness challenge at work and learned that while I thought I was eating healthy, there was more I could be doing. I started eating less processed foods and more fresh produce and healthy fats. I learned to limit my added sugar intake to 20 grams a day. I discovered that the yogurt I was eating daily, and thought was so healthy, had more than the 20 grams of sugar for my daily allowance. I changed to one with only 6 grams of sugar. These small changes overtime, healed my IBS, and I no longer have daily headaches. I lost 16 pounds during the 12- week work wellness challenge, and I have been able to maintain that weight for 11 years.

I learned the difference between unconscious eating and conscious eating. Eating consciously is eating for nourishment (when I am hungry) and without distractions. It is slowing down as I chew my food and noticing the taste, smell, and texture of the food. I can remember several times when I ate so fast and distracted that I didn't even taste my food. This way of eating can result in digestive issues too. Since I have slowed down when I eat, and limited my sugar intake and processed foods, I have more energy and feel good that I am feeding my body with quality nutrition 80% of the time. I still allow myself goodies once in a while, as denying myself can lead to overeating, and I don't want to do that.

So are you an unconscious or conscious eater? Do you eat because you are hungry, tired or under stress?

I have compiled a list of foods that give you energy and foods that zap your energy. The list is not all inclusive, but it gives a good example of each food group. When you can start to incorporate some of these energy foods daily and start to avoid the foods that zap your energy, you will not only nourish your body but your mind and soul as well.

Foods that create energy and nourish:

- *Whole grains-* quinoa, brown rice, wheat, barley, millet, oats. Whole grains are essential to our health, providing fiber, vitamins, phytonutrients and other nutrients that are not available in any other effectively synergistic package. (Synergy is the interaction of two or more nutrients that work together to achieve an effect that each is individually unable to match.) They may reduce the risk of 20 different types of cancer and also benefit the heart and may reduce stroke. They are absorbed slowly, so they give lasting energy.

- *Healthy fats-* walnuts, almonds, seeds, olive oil, avocado, fish. These healthy fats provide Omega-3 fatty acids, which help reduce inflammation, lower risk for heart disease, regulates hormones and neurological function, strengthens immunity and ensure communication between cells.

- *Green vegetables-* dark leafy greens like spinach, kale, Swiss chard, and collard greens. They are rich in antioxidants, which help fight fatigue and stress, and cleanse the body of toxins.

- *Fruits and berries-* contain disease fighting antioxidants and flavonoids, which may reduce the effects of age-related conditions of the brain, such as dementia.

- *Water-* hydrates and removes toxins. We cannot survive without water. When your body is working more efficiently, you have more energy. Drinking water has over 40 benefits (See page 44). It is recommended that you drink half your body weight in ounces, daily. For example, if you weigh 140 pounds, it is recommended that you drink 70 ounces of water daily. Add a slice of lemon or cucumber for flavor, which also helps to detoxify your body.

- *Protein-* hard boiled eggs, nuts, lean meat/poultry, yogurt, cheese. Protein is essential for the body's energy. It helps strengthen muscle and certain body tissues. It is the closest to what is called direct fuel for our bodies and made up of a variety of amino acids. Lack of adequate protein can lead to loss of muscle mass and then starvation.

Foods that zap energy, which can lead to disease:

- *Fried foods and fast food-* These foods are cooked with partially hydrogenated oils, which are oils that have been modified and closely resemble plastic.

- *Processed foods-* crackers, chips, cookies, frozen dinners, lunch meat. These foods are loaded with chemicals and additives.

- *Caffeine-* coffee, soda pop. Caffeine is a stimulant. Too much can give you the shakes, make you irritable and keep you from sleeping. Not enough sleep leaves you tired. Caffeine decreases blood flow to the brain by 30%. This compromises memory and cognitive performance. It stimulates the body to produce stress hormones. It is also addictive.

- *Simple carbohydrates* -sugar and sweeteners like corn syrup, table sugar, honey, molasses. They have a roller coaster effect on the body. Simple Carbs give immediate energy and then a severe crash. It creates an inflammatory response. Too much sugar can lead to 150 health problems, including depression, mood swings, obesity, fatigue, headaches, dizziness, mental confusion, cancer, heart disease, diabetes, and muscle pain, to name a few.

What is one food on the energy food list that you will try today?

What is one food on the zapping energy food list that you will limit tomorrow?

Summary

Proper nutrition provides the nutrients and vitamins our body and mind need for energy and to overcome stress. It also supports a healthy gastrointestinal tract. More than 70% of the immune system is located in the stomach or gut. This is why proper digestion is so important. Eating consciously will aid in proper digestion. Eating nutrient dense foods, (foods that provide energy) and avoiding foods that zap your energy, will bring your body back into balance and help you overcome stress on your mind and body that energy-zapping foods create. You will find that making small changes, like adding a handful of nuts daily, will have a big impact on how you feel. Overtime, you won't miss those energy-zapping foods. And if you overdo on the zapping foods one day, you get to start over the next day. Every day is a new day to start over. I find that if you eat healthy 80% of the time, you will have the energy you need to get through your day, as well as feel good and maintain a healthy weight.

Client Testimonial:

> *I was struggling with eating healthy, stomach issues and anxiety. After working with Sandy, I no longer have stomach issues, and I can better control my anxiety. I needed someone to hold me accountable for eating healthier foods and exercising, and she was there for that. Sandy was very supportive and knowledgeable.*
>
> *Shelby*

THREE

Calming the Crazy
Brain Chatter

In Chapter 1, I mentioned that we have over 60,000 thoughts a day and that it is our thoughts that creates stress. Most of these thoughts are recycled thoughts, which means we are having the same thoughts over and over, day after day. Can you think of a time when you couldn't get something out of your head? This is what I call, "crazy brain chatter". It's when we have obsessive thoughts (worry), or negative self-talk. These both can bring on anxiety, which is a result of worry and stress. This can become an endless cycle.

I have always been a worrier and had negative self-talk at an early age, but I never thought of myself as being anxious. Come to find out, I just didn't know the meaning of it. Anxiety is a symptom of worry and stress and has an emotional and physiological component. That would be me. I discovered that I experience anxiety anytime I speak in front of people. I have feelings of fear, which is an emotional component. Then I notice my heart beating faster, and I break out into a sweat, and my face becomes red, which is a physiological component. Other symptoms I experience when I am worried are stomach aches and headaches. Both of my parents were worriers, so it is no wonder I became one as well.

Worry and negative self-talk can result not only in anxiety, but mental exhaustion, aches and pains, general fatigue, loss of appetite, weight gain, self-medication such as cigarettes or alcohol or wine, and depression.

Being raised in a dysfunctional family, I learned early on that cigarettes and booze worked well to curb stress and anxiety. I remember I was 9 years old when I lit my first cigarette. I think at that time it was out of curiosity, as both of my parents smoked. I thought it tasted nasty, and I hated the smell, but I picked them up again at the age of 16, when my teen years became stressful. I also started to drink on the weekends to escape from my home life.

Both of my parents drank but not excessive, at least not in front of me. My mom drank beer, and my dad liked vodka and squirt. I remember my dad was more of a social drinker, but my mom drank at home. I was a lightweight when it came to alcohol. If I had more than two drinks in a night, I was drunk. When I drank whiskey for the first time, I had to have my boyfriend stop the car and pull over so I could vomit. I tried marijuana, in my teens, but I didn't like how that made me feel, so I passed on that when offered.

I had slowed down my drinking, once I became pregnant with my first son, and I was able to quit smoking "cold turkey" the day I found out I was pregnant with our second son.

I think when you are pre-disposed to addictive behavior and you quit one addiction, it is replaced with another addiction. After I quit smoking, I later became a workaholic. These addictions helped me lessen my anxiety, but once I began my wellness journey, I found healthier ways to deal with anxiety, which I will be sharing in this chapter. Before I do that, I would like to share my stories of when my anxiety spiraled out of control, and I thought I was going crazy.

I can recall two times when my crazy brain chatter almost made me insane. The first time was in 2001, after 16 years of marriage to my high school sweetheart. My husband had been acting distant and cold. He expressed to me that he wasn't sure if he wanted to be married, and he didn't like much about his life at that time. He ended up moving out of our bedroom and then out of our home. Our boys were in their early teens, and I was in a situation I never wanted to be in. I did not want my family split up, as my parent's divorce devastated me at age 17.

I became a basket case. I felt totally rejected by my husband and all I could do was cry day-after- day, for weeks. I had a strong need to be liked by everyone and to be loved. I couldn't stand the thought of not being with my husband again. My obsessive thoughts about our marriage and my negative self-talk (low self-worth) drove me to the point where I thought I was going crazy. I decided to see a psychologist to help me get through this craziness. I needed help to pull myself together.

My psychologist introduced me to the term, "co-dependency" and "dysfunctional family". I learned for the first time that I had a disease called co-dependency, as a result of growing up in an alcoholic family, also known as a dysfunctional family. My behaviors and thoughts started to make sense. I learned that a dysfunctional family didn't support open communication or feelings. I realized my behavior was learned from growing up with secrets, jealousy, the need for control, perfectionism, people pleasing, and enabling, to name a few of the co-dependency characteristics. However, my parents also taught me kindness, compassion, loyalty, strength, love, and an outstanding work ethic. I don't blame my parents for any of my behaviors. I believe that my parents were doing the best they knew how at any given time. I now can see that they too showed symptoms of co-dependency.

I saw my psychologist for a year, and during that time, I discovered that I was a people -pleaser and didn't know how to ask for what I wanted or needed. I became enmeshed with everyone around me and lost sight of who I was. I grew so much during that time. My psychologist introduced me to the concept of self-care and how to start living my own life. I started to put myself first. It was a little uncomfortable at the beginning, but like with anything new, the more I practiced it, the better it felt. I was able to replace my negative self-talk with positive self-talk. My psychologist recommended two books for me to read that I continue to recommend to my friends and clients. The books are, The Woman's Book of Courage and The Woman's Book of Confidence both written by Sue Patton Theole. I still have these books and refer to them whenever I fall back into old bad thought habits.

As for what happened with my marriage? After six months of separation, we decided that we did not want to end our marriage, and my husband moved back home. We have been married now for 36 years. We have been through a lot together with family crises and health issues. These trials and triumphs have kept us together. He seems to find a way to make me laugh, and he tells me that I keep him grounded. Relationships for co-dependents can be difficult to maneuver; however, I am grateful for these life lessons, as they have helped me learn who I am and how to live my own life and allow others to live their life.

The second time I couldn't calm my crazy brain chatter was when my son came to visit me on his 27th birthday, to tell me he was addicted to opioids and wanted help. I told him that was the best birthday present he could have given himself. However, I knew it would be a bumpy road to travel. I helped him call his insurance company and rehab facilities. He was able to get into a weekend detox program that night. However, he did not attend outpatient treatment, and he quickly turned to whiskey instead of opioids to satisfy his addiction. We went through two years of hell. He had several attempts at rehab and several hospitalizations. He lived an hour from us, so I spent every waking minute, and most nights worrying about him. Was he OK? Was he working? How much was he drinking? Did he harm himself again? I became obsessed with his welfare. Since my brother was an alcoholic, I already knew that addiction was a disease, and the drinking was a symptom of his disease. I turned my anger of the disease into compassion for my son, as he didn't want this destructive disease any more than I wanted him to have it.

There is nothing worse than watching your son struggle with this horrible disease and knowing that you have no control over what he does or what happens. The whiskey made him very ill, and within two years of daily drinking, he ended up in the Intensive Care Unit with severe pancreatitis and a feeding tube. He could have died. I had to have the excruciating conversation with him on whether he wanted to be intubated and kept on life support. Thankfully, it did not come to that, and he was discharged from the hospital after three weeks. I was sure that after coming so close to dying, he would not pick up another drink. I was wrong. This just demonstrates how powerful this disease called addiction is. We found out he was drinking again one week after he was out of the hospital. My heart sank. My worrying was uncontrollable. We lost my sister-in-law by suicide at age 28 because of alcoholism. We didn't want to lose our son. So, my husband and I decided to have an intervention with our son, and he agreed to come home to stay with us, so we could help him get the outpatient treatment he needed and attend his AA meetings. He has been sober and in recovery now for five years and is very appreciative of our support and for not giving up on him. We are so grateful that he didn't give up.

It was at one of the rehab centers that I was again reminded of the importance of self-care for family and friends affected by a loved one's drinking. They also recommended that we start our own recovery program, such as personal counseling or a 12 -step program. I took this to heart, as I knew I had to be healthy, mentally, physically and spiritually for me and my family, during this difficult time. I had not been eating well or sleeping well. I had lost weight from not eating, and I knew I had to find something to calm my crazy brain chatter. I decided to join a 12-step program to get the support from people just like me. It is called Al-Anon. I also decided to enroll in a holistic wellness coaching program to become a certified wellness coach. I've always believed that our mind and body work as one and that our thoughts affect our body. I knew this class would teach me how to take better care of myself, holistically (mind, body and spirit) and then allow me to help other women just like me.

Below are some ways you can calm your crazy brain chatter.

1. **_Read inspirational quotes or books_**- We need to feed our mind with healthy nutrition just like our body. Read an inspirational book or positive quotes. I love quotes. Here are some of my favorite quotes: "Look at Life's Challenges not as setbacks but as opportunities to discover who we are." "Life does not get better by Chance; it gets better by Change."

2. **_Stay in the present moment (mindfulness)_**- When worry starts to creep in, reel yourself back to what you were doing at the present moment. Use your five senses to really be in the present moment. I

love to wash dishes. This keeps my mind in the present moment, as I feel the warm, soapy water on my hands. The scrubbing not only washes away the dirt on the dishes but cleanses my soul as well.

3. *Let go*- Let go of that worry and put your faith in your higher power or the universe. Things will most likely work out just fine or better than expected. I say the Serenity Prayer when I need to let go of something that I think I have control over, but I really don't. "God Grant me the Serenity to accept the things I cannot change, the courage to change the things I can and the wisdom to know the difference."

4. *Plan ahead*- If you are worried about an event, like a family reunion that takes place outside, plan ahead and reserve a pavilion.

5. *Read or write an affirmation*- Affirmations are positive phrases or statements that you repeat to yourself. This helps you to manifest what you would rather be experiencing.

6. *Set boundaries*- Learn to say, "No" to those things that will overextend you or that you don't like to do. This will remove any resentment from your head and leave room for peace instead.

7. **Journal**- Write down your thoughts and feelings. Once you get them out of your head, you will feel better.

8. **Release perfectionism**- I always thought that being a perfectionist was a positive trait, until I learned otherwise. Trying to be perfect is putting unrealistic expectations on yourself, and can limit you from living life. I spent many nights unable to sleep because of my perfectionism; replaying what I said and how I wish I would have said it this way instead.

9. **Become aware**- Awareness of your obsessive thoughts or worry is an important step in knowing what tip will be useful for you.

10. **Seek support**- If your crazy brain chatter is just too much to handle, consult with a therapist or wellness coach for additional support. There is nothing wrong with asking for help.

Which of these tips will you try?

Summary

If you find yourself replaying the same thoughts in your head, day after day, you are not alone. The average person has 60,000 thoughts a day and most of them are recycled, which means, they are the same thoughts. I was so relieved to hear that I was not alone. Did you know that 70% of our thoughts are negative? It is these negative thoughts that are causing stress. Have you ever noticed that when you think of one negative thought, you can think of plenty more? This becomes a snowball effect. That is why releasing your negative or obsessive thoughts is so important to your overall health. Worry and negative self-talk can result not only in anxiety, but mental exhaustion, aches and pains, general fatigue, loss of appetite, weight gain, depression or self-medication, which is generally not a healthy choice.

Most of our obsessive thoughts are on things that happened in the past or things that we are trying to predict for the future that will probably never happen. When we worry about tomorrow, we lose the gift of living today. When we worry about the past, which we cannot change, we lose the gift of living today. Living in the past can be good for a short period of time, so we can learn from our mistakes or discover what would work better for us. However, living in the present moment will bring more peace and serenity. You can learn to control your thoughts and calm your crazy brain chatter through awareness and adding in some of the practices or tips that I provided.

Client Testimonial:

> *I was struggling with the ability to say "No" and not feel guilty. I felt abused and pushed around. While working with Sandy, I learned that I am only responsible for MY actions. I gained improved self-esteem and self-confidence and learned to stand up for myself. I am now able to say "No" without feeling guilty, and I realized that I don't have to be the one to always fix everything. My family and co-workers have noticed the positive change in me. I appreciate Sandy's help more than she will ever know.*
>
> *Maria*

FOUR

Recharge through Rest

Sleep is just as important to your energy and overall wellbeing as getting proper nutrition. The body needs sleep to rest and recoup. A good night's sleep (8 hours) has many benefits. Sleep boosts your immune system. It facilitates memory and cognitive reasoning. It imparts a healthy glowing complexion. Sleep keeps your heart healthy. It may prevent cancer by reducing inflammation. Sleep may reduce depression. I think the most important benefit is that it balances hormone levels, including the stress hormone cortisol and growth hormones. Remember, it is our thoughts that bring on stress that revs up cortisol, which then can lead to illness. Sleeping is a way to stop that crazy brain chatter and allow your body to recharge, so you wake up with more energy instead of feeling depleted.

I am sure you know how exhausted you feel when you don't get enough sleep, night after night. That tiredness soon turns into mood swings, whether you realize it or not. But did you know that lack of sleep is directly linked to weight gain? Being overweight or obese has a long list of added health issues. Chronic insomnia can lead to headaches, anxiety, depression, high blood pressure and diabetes. What does your body tell you when you don't get enough sleep?

Getting a good night's sleep has always been a struggle for me. I am highly sensitive and part of that is being a light sleeper. As a child, thunderstorms kept me awake. The noise of the thunder and brightness from the lightening both scared me terribly. It still does to this day. Then when I became a mom, I didn't sleep well, as I laid in bed, half-awake, listening for any noise from our newborn son. Then as the years passed and life became more challenging and busier, it was stress that kept me awake at night. That crazy brain chatter wouldn't stop. I was either worried about a loved one or situation or trying to find solutions to a problem at 2:00am. I had this constant need to help everyone. I could not stand to see my loved ones in pain or struggling with anything. I spent many nights sleepless with worry, especially when my son was drinking heavily and in the hospital with severe pancreatitis. I was worried sick about him literally. My lack of sleep was making me sick. I had constant headaches and stomachaches. I had brain fog. I was irritable. I looked terrible with dark circles under my eyes. But I put on my happy face and told everyone I was doing just fine. However, our bodies can't lie and several years later, my stressful life resulted in Adrenal fatigue also called "burnout".

It wasn't until I enrolled into my wellness coaching class that I understood the importance of sleep and rest. I used to tell myself that I didn't have time to just rest or when I did, I felt guilty, as there were plenty of other things that I felt I should be doing. I discovered tools to help me stop the crazy brain chatter so I could start getting a better night's sleep. Once I put these tools into use, I woke up more refreshed. I had more energy to get through my day. The brain fog and headaches disappeared.

I read about the benefits of Magnesium, and felt this was a healthy way for me to get a better night's sleep, so I started taking the supplement about an hour before I went to bed. Magnesium has over 45 health benefits, but the main reason why I take it is because it is a stress reliever. It also keeps my digestion regular, so I am no longer constipated. Exercise also helps me sleep better and has many other health benefits. I love to Jazzercise. It's so fun and doesn't feel like exercise to me. The other "tools" that help me are keeping a nightly routine to wind down before bed. I will either drink a cup of warm chamomile tea, read an inspirational book or quote, recite the Serenity Prayer, or write in my gratitude journal. If I wake up in the middle of the night with worry, I name all my favorite ice cream flavors, (in my head) and then I can fall back to sleep. This works because it takes my mind off what I was thinking about and puts my focus on something else. Now that I have embraced self-care, my sleep is very important to me.

Here are some recommendations to start a healthy, bedtime routine, so you will fall asleep faster and stay asleep.

1. ***Adjust the heat and lighting in your room for comfort***- The darker and cooler, the better

2. ***Cut out all noise***- Close windows or doors or use ear plugs

3. ***Do not oversleep***- Go to bed and wake up at the same time each day

4. ***Shut off electronics***- Stop looking at TV screen or phone at least one hour before bedtime

5. ***Meditate***- Meditation recharges our mind, body and soul. There are many free guided meditation apps. Meditating for as little as 10 minutes is beneficial.

6. ***Use aromatherapy***- Lavender linen spray on your bedding causes relaxation or use lavender oil in a diffuser in your bedroom to bring calmness

7. ***Journal***- Write down your thoughts before bed or if you wake up in the middle of the night, so you can get them out of your head and get back to sleep.

8. ***Unwind before bed***- Listen to soothing music or take a warm bath with Epsom salt and lavender oil

9. ***Avoid heavy meals***- Eating before going to bed may cause digestive issues, insomnia and possibly weight gain. Don't eat anything at least two hours before bedtime.

10. ***Make a "to do list"*** – Write down what you need to do for the next day, so your mind is not stuck on the activities that need to get done.

There are many sleep aids available, but be cautious of over-the -counter or prescribed medications. These medications may induce sleep, but they are extremely addictive and provide short-term relief. They can also make you feel drowsy during the day. Here are few natural remedies to help you get to sleep:

1. Milk with honey
2. Warm tea with Chamomile or Lavender
3. Melatonin supplement
4. Magnesium supplement
5. Water as it restores normal sleep rhythm
6. Passion Flower (herb)
7. Lavender
8. Lemon balm
9. Himalayan Salt lamp- this improves air quality, mood and improves sleep. Keep one in your bedroom next to your bed.

Please consult with your physician before trying any new supplement or herb, as these may occasionally interfere with other medications you might be taking.

What new bedtime activity or remedy will you try tonight?

Summary

Lack of sleep can cause mental and physical exhaustion, as well as a host of illness and disease, including a weakened immune system, memory loss, mood changes, hormone function, diabetes, weight gain, heart disease, and low sex drive. I think women are finally understanding the significance of a good night's sleep and accepting the fact that they can't maintain their level of busyness and resume the role of Superwoman. Most women feel guilty if they take a few minutes to rest. I was reminded by my Wellness Instructor that we are human beings, not human doers. It is OK to just be; to sit for a few minutes, to relax, to say, "NO", and get eight hours of sleep, without feeling guilty. Our bodies and brain need this time of rest, so it can recharge and repair itself.

What is causing your lack of sleep? Are you overextending yourself? Is it too noisy in your room? Are your thoughts running wild? Once you become aware of the root cause of your sleep deprivation, you can use the tool that is best for your circumstance. Once you start to sleep better, you will feel better and be able to perform your daily tasks with more energy and clarity.

Client Testimonial:

> *Sandy was a great guide and listener in the various challenges I presented to her that she in return, helped guide me through to a solution. She was always patient and asked questions that helped me come to my own conclusions, helping me find my own inner guide. Her valuable knowledge and insight were much appreciated and welcomed.*
>
> *Tracey*

CONCLUSION

You have now discovered that stress can affect your health in many ways. A little stress is good for you, as it helps you take action and provides personal growth, but when you are experiencing high levels of stress daily, it can be very detrimental to your health. As discussed, stress can harm your immune system, cause depression, heart disease, anxiety, exhaustion, insomnia, digestive issues, headaches, stroke and even death. This is very scary, but the good news is that now you have many tools to help you overcome your day-to-day stress.

My hope is that I provided you with enough resources and hope for better days ahead, without overloading you with too much information. When I was at my highest level of stress, I wanted something easy to read and understand to help me take control of my health and my life. This book was created with that in mind. I wanted to share information that can be used as a quick reference guide. The stress we face as co-dependents can be overbearing at times. Stress comes at us constantly in all directions; environmentally (chemicals in our food and water, noise pollution); physically (jobs, running errands, taking care of family) and emotionally (worry, anxiety, sleep deprivation). Most of the time, we don't even realize the amount of stress we are enduring. However, I know from personal experience that taking small, healthy, steps can have a huge impact on our overall health and wellbeing. My ultimate wish is that you learn to embrace self-care and start to put your wellbeing first, when appropriate.

Once you incorporate some of the easy tips throughout this guide, you will be amazed at how you will start to have more energy, find peace and take better control of your thoughts. We are all unique individuals, so listen to your body and find what works best for you. I am in awe at the abundance of healthy alternatives offered in place of or in combination with Western medicine. Mother Nature provides us with an endless supply of different healthy remedies to overcome stress in our lives. But as a gentle reminder, please consult your physician before taking any supplements or herbs, especially if you are on medication.

As I mentioned in my introduction, my wellness philosophy is "**Self-care is not selfish, it is essential.**" I also feel very strongly that our life's journey is not meant to be traveled alone, and asking for help is not a weakness but a strength. I sought out a psychologist in my darkest of days, and now I have my own wellness coach, who helps me move forward when I feel stuck or overwhelmed.

Asking for help takes practice, just like anything new you undertake. Should you feel like you need additional support, I am here for you. Turn to the Bonus Section to learn about my offer for a free consultation.

Wishing you health & happiness,

Sandy

WORKBOOK

Notes

WORKBOOK

Notes

Benefits of Drinking Water

Drinking water is one of the easiest things you can do to improve your health. We can't survive without water. Our bodies are made of more than 70% water. Not enough water (dehydration) can cause minor to severe symptoms, including sluggishness, fainting, headache, confusion, difficulty breathing, decreased urine output and kidney failure.

There are over 40 reasons to drink water. Here are some of the major benefits of water:

1. Flushes out toxins and excess fat from the body
2. Keeps skin moist and healthy, minimizing wrinkles
3. Controls appetite, keeping the body leaner
4. Makes nutrients from food move throughout your body
5. Main source of energy
6. It holds your cells together properly
7. Helps prevent arthritis and back pain by keeping joints healthy
8. Aids your body to process the food you eat and helps relieve constipation
9. Helps keep blood flowing through arteries easily, reducing your chance of experiencing heart attack or stroke

10. Assists with healthy brain function, reducing depression, anxiety and stress
11. Restores normal sleep rhythm
12. Reverses addictive urges, including caffeine, alcohol and some drugs
13. Increases your attention span
14. Decreases premenstrual cramps and hot flashes
15. Helps you fight off colds and flu with a stronger immune system
16. Helps prevent memory loss as we age
17. Aids in eye health
18. Essential for the body's cooling system
19. Helps circulate oxygen in your body
20. Assists with production of all hormones that keep your body functioning properly

Affirmations

Positive affirmations are positive phrases you can repeat to yourself that describe what you want to experience, feel or receive.

I am receiving all that is good.

I am worthy of love and happiness.

I respect others to live their own life, while I respect me as I live mine.

I am living a life of abundance.

I am grateful for this healthy and beautiful body.

I choose positive self- talk in difficult situations.

I am healing my mind and body with loving thoughts.

I choose faith over fear.

I choose to embrace self-care without feeling guilty.

I forgive myself and others.

The Energy Checklist

This energy checklist will help you take a closer look at what parts of your lifestyle may be affecting your energy level. Go through this checklist anytime you are feeling tired or sluggish to discover where your low energy level is coming from and what steps you can take to feel your best.

1. Am I sleeping well?

    a. Journal to get thoughts out of your head
    b. Stick to a peaceful bedtime routine
    c. Use aromatherapy such as lavender linen spray

2. What have I had to eat lately?

    a. Focus on foods that bring you energy like green veggies (i.e., spinach, kale, broccoli), whole grains/seeds (i.e., quinoa, brown rice), healthy fats (i.e., nuts or olive oil) and lean protein (i.e., chicken)
    b. Limit foods and drinks that zap energy such as soda, sugar and processed foods
    c. Take time to eat slowly, savoring your food without distractions like TV

3. What kind of movement have I gotten?

    a. Take a walk -10 minutes a couple times a day

b.　Get up and stretch your arms and legs

4.　Am I drinking enough water?

    a.　Add lemon or cucumber slices or fresh fruit for flavor if you have a hard time drinking water

    b.　Aim for at least 64 oz. of water. Fill a 20 oz. water bottle three times during your day and take it with you wherever you go

    c.　Decaf herbal tea counts, since it is not a diuretic like caffeinated drinks

5.　When was the last time I had "me time"?

    a.　Get a massage

    b.　Read a book

    c.　Take a yoga class

    d.　Take a bath with Epsom salts and lavender or orange essential oil

6.　Have I been outside in nature?

    a.　Connect with nature for some serenity and experience your senses of sight, smell, hearing and touch

    b.　Try a grounding exercise by going barefoot outdoors

MY FAVORITE EASY RECIPES

These recipes were shared with me, and they have become some of my favorite recipes. I am all about easy. As you can see by reading their nutritional values, they are packed full of healthy nutrients, which guard against illness. I love walnuts for their flavor but also because they share double duty as a healthy fat and protein. You can omit the walnuts, if you are not a fan of them, or substitute with your favorite nut.

Sinless Cookies

2 Ripe Bananas
1 Cup Quick Oats
1 Heaping Tablespoon of Natural Peanut Butter
1/2 Cup of Dark Chocolate Chips
(add a little Vanilla or Honey)

Mash bananas in a bowl, add the remaining ingredients.
Mix until blended well. Place on cookie sheet and bake for
13-15 minutes on 350 degrees

Makes about eight cookies.

Nutritional values: protein, fiber, potassium, manganese,
iron, zinc, selenium, magnesium, anti-inflammatories,
Vitamins C & B6 and phytonutrients

Protein & Fruit Smoothie

8 oz water or unsweetened almond milk

1 scoop protein powder (avoid whey powder)

1 cup fresh or frozen berries

1 half banana

2 tablespoons ground flax seed meal

1 teaspoon Cinnamon, Ginger or Turmeric

2 ice cubes, if preferred colder

Combine all ingredients in blender and blend well. Pour into a tumbler and enjoy as a meal or a snack.

Nutritional values: protein, calcium using almond milk, antioxidants, fiber, Omega 3 fatty acids, Amino acids, Potassium, Vitamins C & E, Riboflavin, Iron, Niacin, Folate, Carotenoids and anti-inflammatories

Energy Bars

1 20 oz can pineapple (crushed) in own juice
½ cup crushed almonds
2 cups rolled oats
3 scoops hemp, soy or rice/pea protein powder
1 cup chopped dried fruit
1 ½ teaspoons cinnamon

Preheat oven to 200 degrees. Combine all ingredients. Spread in 13 x 9 inch pan brushed with expeller-pressed canola or almond oil. Bake for 90 minutes. Cool and slice. Store in refrigerator.

Nutritional values: fiber, Vitamins C & E, protein, Omega 3 fatty acids, magnesium, Potassium, Zinc, Copper, Selenium, Thiamine, Manganese, Amino acids, Iron, Folate, Riboflavin, Carotenoids, anti-inflammatories

Green Beans with Olives, Sun-dried Tomatoes and Walnuts

½ cup Walnuts, chopped

1 tablespoon extra-virgin olive oil or oil from sun-dried tomatoes

¾ pound green beans, fresh with ends trimmed

¼ cup mixed olives, pitted and chopped or sliced

1 ½ tablespoons lemon juice

2 tablespoons sun-dried tomatoes, chopped

½ teaspoon sea salt

Step 1

Place walnuts in a large skillet over medium heat. Cook for 5 minutes or until toasted and fragrant, stirring frequently. Remove from skillet and set aside.

Step 2

Heat oil in same skillet over medium-high heat. Add green beans and cook for 5 minutes or until crisp-tender, stirring frequently.

Step3

Add olives, tomatoes, lemon juice and salt. Cook for a minute or two until all ingredients are hot.

Step 4

Sprinkle with walnuts and serve

Nutritional values: protein, fiber, Vitamins C, K & A, Omega 3 fatty acids, magnesium, potassium, zinc, Copper, selenium, thiamine, manganese, amino acids, iron, folate, riboflavin, carotenoids, anti-inflammatories, anti-oxidants, calcium

Quinoa with Apples and Walnuts Salad

1 cup red quinoa, rinsed well

¼ cup orange juice

1 tablespoon lemon juice

1 tablespoon olive oil

2 tablespoons chopped fresh cilantro

2 tablespoons chopped fresh mint

½ teaspoon salt

Pinch black pepper

2 apples, cored and finely chopped

½ cup chopped walnuts

¼ cup thinly sliced scallion or finely chopped red onion
(optional)

4 cups spring salad mix

Step 1

Cook quinoa according to package directions

Step 2

Combine orange juice, lemon juice, oil, cilantro, mint and
salt & pepper in large bowl

Step 3

Stir in the cooked quinoa, apples, walnuts and scallion or onion. Toss well to combine. Place on top of spring salad mix – divide onto to four plates.

Nutritional values: protein, fiber, Vitamins C, K & A, Omega 3 fatty acids, magnesium, potassium, zinc, Copper, selenium, thiamine, manganese, amino acids, iron, folate, riboflavin, flavonoids, beta-carotene, anti-inflammatories, anti-oxidants, calcium

Sweet Potatoes with Cinnamon and Walnuts

2 sweet potatoes, washed and scrubbed

1 tablespoon olive oil

1 teaspoon ground cinnamon

2 Tablespoons walnuts, chopped

Preheat oven to 350 degrees. Place cookie sheet lined with tin foil to catch drippings. Rub sweet potatoes with olive oil then poke potatoes with a fork.

Bake potatoes on over rack for 80 minutes or until soft.

Cut open potatoes, sprinkle with cinnamon and top with walnuts.

Nutritional values: protein, fiber, Vitamins C & A, Omega 3 fatty acids, magnesium, potassium, zinc, Copper, selenium, thiamine, manganese, amino acids, iron, folate, riboflavin, flavonoids, beta-carotene, anti-inflammatories, anti-oxidants, calcium

Quinoa with Shrimp

1 ¼ cups sliced zucchini (2 medium size zucchini)
1 garlic clove (minced)
1 tablespoon olive oil
3 oz. shrimp (peeled and veined)
Pinch coarse salt
Pinch red pepper flakes
1 ½ teaspoon oregano or ½ dried
1 cup halved grape tomatoes
½ cup quinoa cooked

Heat olive oil in a skillet over medium heat. Add sliced zucchini. Cook until zucchini starts to turn golden, 2 4 minutes. Add garlic clove and shrimp. Cook until shrimp start to turn pink about 2 minutes. Add salt and red pepper flakes, oregano and grape tomatoes. Cook until tomatoes soften, 2 minutes. Serve over ½ cup cooked quinoa.

Serves 4- can substitute chicken for shrimp.

Nutritional values: protein, fiber, Vitamins C & B12, Omega 3 fatty acids, magnesium, potassium, zinc, copper, selenium, choline manganese, iron, folate, riboflavin, flavonoids, beta-carotene, anti-inflammatories, anti-oxidants, calcium

Turkey Fiesta Soup

1 tablespoon olive oil

1 onion chopped

1 small jalapeno pepper, seeded and finely chopped (wear plastic gloves when handling)

1 medium zucchini, chopped

2 teaspoons ground cumin

½ teaspoon chili powder

1 pound 98% fat-free ground turkey

1 package (32 oz.) low-sodium chicken broth

1 can (14.5 oz.) diced tomatoes

1 can (15 oz.) black beans, rinsed and drained

1 cup frozen corn kernels

½ cup chopped cilantro

½ cup avocado chopped

6 tablespoons shredded cheddar cheese

Step 1

In a large saucepan, heat the oil over medium-high heat. Cook onion and jalapeno, stirring occasionally for 5 minutes or until lightly browned. Stir in zucchini and cook for 10 minutes or until lightly browned. Add turkey and cook, stirring to break up with a spoon until no longer pink.

Step 2

Stir in the broth, tomatoes with juice, beans corn, cumin, and chili powder. Bring to a boil over high heat. Reduce heat to low and simmer for 20 minutes or until liquid has reduced by one-quarter. Remove from heat.

Step 3

Stir in the cilantro. Divide into bowls. Sprinkle each serving with a spoonful of avocado and 1 tablespoon of cheese.

Nutritional values: protein, fiber, Vitamins C, A, B6 & B12, Omega 3 fatty acids, magnesium, potassium, zinc, copper, selenium, thiamin, manganese, iron, folate, riboflavin, flavonoids, beta-carotene, anti-inflammatories, anti-oxidants, calcium and phosphorus

Greek Chicken Thighs with Artichokes and Olives

8 bone-in skin on chicken thighs (about 2.5 pounds)

¼ teaspoon sea salt

¼ teaspoon ground black pepper

1 medium onion, sliced

2 ½ tablespoons extra virgin olive oil

3 large garlic cloves, finely chopped

1 can (15 oz.) water-packed artichoke hearts, well drained

4 oz. mixed pitted Greek olives

1 ½ cups low-sodium chick broth

2 tablespoons fresh chopped oregano leaves or 2 teaspoons dried

1 large lemon, sliced into thin rounds

2 tablespoons water

Step 1

Trim any excess fat from chicken thighs. Season chicken with salt, pepper and garlic.

Step2

Heat 1 ½ tablespoons of olive oil in a large wide skillet over medium heat. When oil is hot add the chicken skin side down. Cook until skin is crisp and golden brown. Move the chicken thighs to a plate or rimmed baking sheet.

Step 3

To the same pan, add onions and cook until softened. Add chopped garlic and cook 1 minute. Add drained artichoke hearts, olives, broth and remaining 1 tablespoon of olive oil and oregano. Add the chicken thighs back in to the pan and top with lemon slices.

Step 4

Bring the mixture to a strong simmer, put a lid on and reduce the heat to medium low. Simmer over low heat for 13 minutes or until the thighs reach an internal temperature of 165 degrees with measured with a digital thermometer.

To serve, place the chicken thighs in shallow pan and pour the vegetable and jus over the top.

Makes 4 servings

Nutritional values: protein, fiber, Vitamins K, C, A, B6, Omega 3 fatty acids, magnesium, potassium, zinc, selenium, manganese, folate, anti-inflammatories, anti-oxidants, calcium and niacin

FREE CONSULTATION
WITH SANDY SONIER

In this private coaching session, we will discuss your biggest energy challenges and uncover step-by-step ways to get you from where you are to where you want to be. You will come away from this session feeling refreshed and restored.

Contact me via my website https://sandysholisticwellness.com or my email sandy.inspiredliving@gmail.com to schedule your free consultation.

Client Testimonial:

"After each coaching session, Sandy leaves you with a feeling of a safe sense of real authentic support. She guides you on a journey in a clear concise way and she really brings out the very best in you. The results that have been there with you all along. A-Ha moment after A-ha moment, sudden powerful shifts in your thinking and you will also always feel completely heard.

Sandy's kind-hearted smile and light-hearted humor makes it that much easier to bond and connect with her.

If you feel stuck in any part of your life, I can assure you that Sandy will gently guide you to explore and experience different aspects and solutions and you can then enjoy the feelings of total confidence as you see your life unfold for the better all the while accomplishing mile stones that you never even thought possible.

For that Sandy I am truly grateful,
Thank you so much,"
Gill

Printed in the United States
by Baker & Taylor Publisher Services